Confirmation

BIBLE READINGS FOR SPECIAL TIMES

...for those times when we want to hear God's word speaking to us clearly

Mike Starkey

Text copyright © Mike Starkey 2006
The author asserts the moral right
to be identified as the author of this work

Published by
The Bible Reading Fellowship
First Floor, Elsfield Hall
15–17 Elsfield Way, Oxford OX2 8FG

ISBN-10 1 84101 494 X
ISBN-13 978 1 84101 494 4

First published 2006
10 9 8 7 6 5 4 3 2 1 0

Acknowledgments
Scripture quotations are taken from the Holy Bible, New International
Version, copyright © 1973, 1978, 1984 by International Bible Society,
are used by permission of Hodder & Stoughton Limited. All rights
reserved. 'NIV' is a registered trademark of International Bible Society.
UK trademark number 1448790.

A catalogue record for this book is available from the British Library

Printed by Gutenberg Press, Tarxien, Malta

Introduction

Confirmation is one of the significant milestones along the Christian journey. To 'confirm' means to make firm, to fulfil, strengthen, or reassert strongly. At my confirmation I confirm the promises that were made at my baptism. For most of us, these promises were made for us, early in our lives. Confirmation now means owning them for myself, publicly declaring that I am a follower of Jesus Christ and that I want my faith in Jesus to shape my values and priorities.

In confirmation, I complete the process of initiation into full church membership which began at my baptism. I become a full member of both the universal Church (the Church throughout the world and throughout history), and also of a particular church—my local church, and the denomination it belongs to. It might mean I can now share in areas of church life that I couldn't previously, and start to take on new responsibilities in the church.

Confirmation is also a kind of commissioning for active service. The bishop lays his hands on my head and prays for God's empowering presence in my life, to keep me strong in the faith and equip me to live for God in the world.

But not everybody has good experiences of confirmation. A church leader once confided to me how he dreads confirmations, as they have effectively become a 'passing-out ceremony' for young people in his church. As soon as they reach secondary school age they all dutifully get confirmed, and that is the last time they are ever seen in church. Plenty of people look back on their own confirmation as a dull ritual that their parents or grandparents expected them to go through, and their confirmation classes as a meaningless chore. Some people were confirmed as part of a 'job lot' in a school where there was an expectation that everybody would be confirmed, irrespective of their faith commitment.

This is far from ideal. Confirmation should be a special and joyful time, a time when I embrace a faith of my own with passion; when I make a public declaration of my faith in the presence of friends and family; when I receive a fresh empowering from God; and when I look forward with excitement to discovering more of my own skills and gifts, and where I can best use them.

It is my hope that these Bible readings and meditations will be a helpful companion for people approaching confirmation, and those who have recently been confirmed. They could, for example, be read one a day in the four weeks running up to the confirmation service. Some people may prefer to dot around in the book, as different themes grab their attention. That's fine!

In particular, I hope that any who may have found themselves pushed towards confirmation by other people's expectations will start to become excited about their confirmation as they read. And I hope that anybody who anticipates their confirmation being as dry as dust will find a few cobwebs being blown away.

The 24 readings are intended as stand-alone reflections, although in some cases a particular reading continues a train of thought from the previous one. Those who are interested in the overall scheme might like to know that they are grouped under four broad themes:

- Christian discipleship
- The church and my place in it
- The confirmation service
- Looking to the future

The limitation of a booklet such as this is, of course, that it only allows for 'bite-size' reflections on some fairly massive issues. I hope you will be stimulated to explore some of the issues raised in much greater depth in other ways. A good place to start would be to ask for a Study Bible as a confirmation gift.

All Bible quotations are taken from the New International Version.

MARK 1:19–20 (ABRIDGED)

Mentor and apprentice

When [Jesus] had gone a little farther, he saw James... and his brother John in a boat, preparing their nets. Without delay he called them, and they left their father Zebedee in the boat with the hired men and followed him.

We all have heroes and role models. Movie stars, sports personalities, authors, business gurus—we love to follow their comings and goings. We may even emulate their lifestyles, attitudes and dress. And it's not only teenagers who do this. I remember one old Methodist minister who grew his hair to shoulder-length so that he'd look like the 18th-century church leaders he admired! Why do we do it? Because we're gripped by a person we admire, and want to become more like them. Back in ancient Israel, students learned by following their teacher around and imitating him in everything. And the name given to these students? 'Disciples.' The word means an apprentice, somebody who has a mentor.

Jesus walked along the shore of the Sea of Galilee, calling a select group of people to be his disciples. He was calling them to follow him and get to know him intimately: watching, listening, learning from his teaching and example. And the call to discipleship goes out to anybody who is ready to follow Jesus today. All who offer themselves for confirmation are saying 'yes' to having Jesus as their mentor, walking with him, spending time with him, learning to see the world as he sees it.

James and John dropped their nets and set off into an unknown future. Discipleship means going on a journey that might feel new and risky. But it's a journey in the company of one we trust, who will accompany us every step of the way.

Jesus calls me to be a disciple. How does that make me feel?

MARK 10:43–45

Learning to serve

*'Whoever wants to become great among you must be
your servant, and whoever wants to be first must be slave
of all. For even the Son of Man did not come to be served,
but to serve.'*

Being a Christian means discipleship—having Jesus as my mentor. And we saw Jesus calling James and John to be disciples. So from that day on, they lived happily ever after? Hardly! Not long after Jesus has called them, we find them arguing about who should have the most prominence, which of them is the greatest disciple.

Jesus has to explain that they've missed the point entirely. Being a disciple is not a kind of spiritual promotion. It's not like being elected to the governing body—it's more like being given the mop and bucket. Disciples of Jesus are called to serve others.

The same is still true for disciples today, as the confirmation service reminds us. It's tempting to think of confirmation as being about 'my' faith, 'my' spirituality. But that's to start at the wrong end. The call to be a disciple is a call to become more like Jesus, to serve others as Jesus did. Sometimes we may be called way beyond our own comfort zones.

We can't say we haven't been warned. As Jesus points out to the first disciples (including James and John), anybody who wants to follow him must deny themselves and carry a cross (Mark 8:34). When Jesus tells us to love others, he's not saying we have to work up warm, fuzzy feelings of affection. He's talking about love as a choice we make: to do loving things for people, even those we find it hard to like.

Discipleship isn't an easy option. But, as James and John found, it is the adventure of a lifetime.

Jesus calls me to serve others. What might that look like in practice?

MATTHEW 6:9

Intimacy with God

'This, then, is how you should pray: "Our Father in heaven,
hallowed be your name…"'

As Jesus' first disciples lived, ate and worked alongside him, one thing became clear: Jesus, their master and mentor, prioritized quality time with God. It was Jesus' intimate relationship with his heavenly Father that energized his whole life and ministry.

So one of the disciples asks Jesus to teach him the secret of this intimacy. How should he pray? In response, Jesus teaches his disciples the prayer we call the Lord's Prayer. Some of us have recited these words since childhood, a familiar formula, which begins 'Our Father' and ends with 'for ever and ever, Amen'. But it's doubtful that Jesus would have intended his disciples to pray the prayer this way—by rote. Rather, I suspect he intended his words to be a checklist for prayer, outlining areas that are essential to building intimacy with God. We praise God for his greatness; we pray for the transformation of our world; we pray for our bodily needs, and acknowledge our dependence on God's provision; we pray for forgiveness and recognize our need to forgive others; we ask God to help us not to be blown off course by temptations too strong for us to bear.

Houseplants thrive when they have water and sunlight. When they are neglected, they wither. The same is true of relationships with other people, and also with God. They thrive only when they are given the time and attention they deserve. And the heart of building any strong relationship is communication. Jesus' disciples learned from him to prioritize communication with God. At my confirmation I tell the world that I want intimacy with God to be the number one priority in my life, as it was for Jesus.

What priority do I give to prayer in my daily routine?

LUKE 15:20

The loving Father

But while he was still a long way off, his father saw him and was filled with compassion for him; he ran to his son, threw his arms around him and kissed him.

It's a heartwarming parable—the prodigal son reunited with his father—but it's one that would have shocked its first hearers. The story starts with a young man going to his father and asking for his share of the inheritance—what he'd get when his father was dead. Effectively, he's saying, 'Dad, I want you dead now.' In a culture where parents are due special respect, it's the ultimate insult.

Jewish law at the time didn't allow children to sell family land until after their father's death. The son cashes in his share straight away, adding to the insult by breaking the law too. It's a personal tragedy and a public humiliation for the father. Then the son returns home, penniless. How will the father react? Jesus' hearers might have expected him to slap the son across the face and drive him out of the house, or formally cut him off from the community.

But not this father. He is already desperately searching the horizon for his boy to return home. Middle Eastern men in long robes never ran in public, because it was considered degrading. But this father hitches up his robes and runs out to meet his son. He kisses the boy who wanted him dead, broke the law, humiliated him and now comes home smelling of pigs!

So many people are held back in prayer by a wrong picture of God, as distant or harsh, so Jesus tells his disciples to pray to God as Father. He loves us more than we can possibly imagine, whatever we have been or done. This is the central motivation of a disciple, which we affirm at our confirmation. It all centres on a restored relationship with a loving heavenly Father.

How does my image of God compare with the father in Jesus' story?

PSALM 104:1a, 10, 12

Praying as I can

Praise the Lord, O my soul... He makes springs pour water into the ravines; it flows between the mountains... The birds of the air nest by the waters; they sing among the branches.

We have seen that intimacy with God is deepened as we take time to pray. We also found that some people struggle in prayer because they have a wrong image of God. It's hard to be intimate with somebody we see as bitter or judgmental.

Others of us struggle not so much because of a wrong image of God, but because of a wrong idea of prayer itself. Over the years, we may have picked up an idea of prayer as kneeling silently at the bedside, hands pressed together; or silently sitting in a cold church; or, at the other extreme, shouting loudly in a room full of noisy fellow believers.

The fact is that God made each of us different, with different personalities, different cultural backgrounds and tastes. Some leaders are keen to tell people the 'right' way to pray. But there isn't a right way to pray. In Jesus' day, most people prayed standing up, eyes open, hands raised. The psalmist who wrote today's reading clearly loved to pray in scenes of stunning natural beauty. Some people like their senses engaged as they pray; others crave solitude and silence. Some find they are helped by prayer in small groups; others find that music leads into prayer. Some are energized by the life of the mind, and find a stretching Bible study a good lead-in to prayer.

Jesus' early disciples were a diverse bunch, and we are too. Don't worry if the next person doesn't pray the way you do. What matters is that you pray in a way that enables you to connect with God.

I need to pray as I can, not as I can't.

LUKE 11:9

Praying for others

'So I say to you: Ask and it will be given to you; seek and you will find; knock and the door will be opened to you.'

Prayer is communication with God, and a real breakthrough comes in private prayer when I find a style of prayer that works for me. Prayer isn't only about me and my needs, though. It's also about the needs of the world. It should include intercession, praying for other people and situations. But why should we pray for others? If God knows what they need, why do we have to tell him?

Perhaps part of our problem is a wrong understanding of how God operates. The Bible tells us that God is almighty and omnipotent. For us, those qualities may evoke images of an autocratic ruler whose word is law: a Henry VIII, Stalin or Saddam. If that sort of ruler makes up his mind, then his will is going to prevail, regardless of anybody else. Maybe a better image is of God as a caring head of a major corporation. He has supreme authority— the buck stops with him. He has a firm vision for the company, but is flexible on how it is achieved. He is the sort of leader who loves to draw others into the process. He listens to others' opinions, and lets them shape the final outcome.

Astonishing as it may seem, God wants to involve us in the implementation of his purposes. You and I can actually affect outcomes by our prayers. The great church leader John Wesley once claimed, 'God does nothing except in answer to prayer.' That may be overstating it a bit, but you can see his point: God uses our prayers to change things in the real world. If we pray, things happen. Then, as I pray for people and situations, it may be that God prods me to become part of the answer to my own prayer. Intercession and action are close cousins!

Which people or situations will I intercede for on a regular basis?

JOHN 1:43, 45a

Passing it on

The next day Jesus decided to leave for Galilee. Finding Philip, he said to him, 'Follow me.' Philip found Nathanael and told him, 'We have found the one Moses wrote about in the Law, and about whom the prophets also wrote...'

One of the people called by Jesus to be a disciple is Philip, a young man from a small village on the north shore of the Sea of Galilee. The first thing Philip does is to run and tell his friend Nathanael about the extraordinary figure he has just met.

A disciple is somebody who calls other people to be disciples too. Some of Jesus' last recorded words to his disciples are, 'Go and make disciples of all nations' (Matthew 28:19). They did just that, and the world was changed. At my confirmation, I pledge to share the good news of Jesus with others, by word and example.

For some of us, the idea of talking to others about Jesus fills us with dread. It may evoke images of missionaries in pith helmets, or people standing on street corners and shouting at passers-by. The simple fact is that we all enthuse about whatever excites us. I was shopping in my local supermarket when one of the staff bounded up to me. 'What do you reckon?' he asked. 'I'd say two-nil to England!' It was inconceivable to him that I wouldn't be interested in that evening's European Cup game.

Sharing my faith isn't about technique or temperament. It's about being gripped by something that excites me. The most significant person in history arrives in a sleepy village and invites Philip to follow him. He offers to be his mentor and friend. How can Philip not enthuse about it to others? My confirmation is a great opportunity to share exciting news about something that really matters to me, with friends, family and colleagues.

Is my enthusiasm for Jesus as infectious as Philip's?

ACTS 16:13–14 (ABRIDGED)

Whole-life discipleship

We went outside the city gate to the river… sat down and began to speak to the women who had gathered there. One of those listening was a woman named Lydia, a dealer in purple cloth from the city of Thyatira, who was a worshipper of God.

Perhaps the idea of discipleship sounds daunting. After all, the original twelve called by Jesus left their old lives behind and spent all their time with him. Surely, we're not all called to give up our homes and livelihoods and become nuns or travelling evangelists? It's true: the first disciples were in a privileged position. They uniquely experienced quality time with Jesus, to equip them for the building of his Church. You and I are called to share important aspects of their discipleship (spending time with Jesus, learning to see the world as he sees it, learning to serve others). But in other ways, our calling is clearly different from theirs.

Perhaps a better discipleship role model for most of us is somebody like Lydia. A Turkish woman, she lived in the city of Philippi (northern Greece), and worked as a rep for a foreign fashion wholesaler. She owned a sizable house, which doubled as a shop for selling the famous purple-dyed clothes from her home town of Thyatira. She already had some sort of faith in God, but one day she met Paul and found faith in Jesus Christ.

What happened next? Did she give up her job and join Paul on the road as a preacher? No; she stayed put, opened her home to Paul and his fellow travellers and shared her faith with her household. For most of us, the call to discipleship is a call to follow Jesus in our homes and workplaces—seeing them with new eyes, as places where we are called to serve others and share our faith.

I follow Jesus not by escaping from my home, workplace and community, but living for him in them.

ACTS 2:38a

Faith and baptism

Peter replied, 'Repent and be baptized, every one of you, in the name of Jesus Christ.'

What is the starting point for discipleship? The answer to that is obvious: being a Christian. But what is a Christian? The answer will vary, depending on who you ask! For some people, a Christian is somebody brought up in a 'Christian' country. For a high proportion of these people, being 'Christian' is clearly an accident of birth, rather than a matter of real conviction.

Some talk of being 'a good Christian', meaning a person who tries to live a moral life. Of course, the Christian life does include a moral dimension, but it is misleading to talk as if Christianity and good behaviour are the same thing. If a Christian slips up morally, that in itself doesn't stop them being a Christian. And people of other faiths—or none—can have high ideals and live moral lives. For others, being a Christian means going to church, but here too the overlap is not exact. In my own church, a good many of those who attend services wouldn't describe themselves as practising Christians. They are still 'dipping their toe in the water'. On the other hand, some devout Christians may, at least temporarily, drop out of Sunday worship due to bad church experiences.

A good summary of what it means to be a Christian is provided by Peter, as he speaks to the crowds in Jerusalem at Pentecost: 'Repent and be baptized.' Repentance means literally 'turning our lives round', turning from a life centred on myself and towards a life centred on God in Jesus Christ. Baptism is the outward sign of the inner change. Faith and baptism are the entry points to the Christian faith, so both of them are essential precursors to confirmation.

Is my faith more than an accident of birth, a set of values, or a Sunday habit?

JOHN 4:42b

The rescue operation

'Now we have heard for ourselves, and we know that this man really is the Saviour of the world.'

One of the main titles given to Jesus in the New Testament is 'Saviour'. From start to finish, Christianity is a rescue operation. What are we saved from? The church's baptism service contains a neat summary: we are saved from 'sin, the world and the devil'. In this section we shall look briefly at the first two, and the third in the next section.

- *Sin:* This can mean broken relationships, and human rebellion against God, as well as the wrong things we do. Sometimes sin is seen as an alien force that takes over its victims (rather like the monster in the film *Alien*). New Testament writers picture sin as an enemy out to destroy us—or at least to hold us back from the fullness of life that God wants to give. That is why we talk about Jesus 'conquering sin'. On the cross, all the worst aspects of human nature are dumped on to Jesus and put to death, so we can be freed from them.
- *The world:* Sometimes Bible writers talk about not being conformed to 'the world'. They mean pressures from our culture, and even friends and family, that pull us away from God; pressures to adopt values and lifestyles that aren't in line with what God wants for us, to downplay our faith or compromise our values.

The biblical picture of human nature is of a battleground. Sin means we are weakened from within, while we are assailed with all sorts of pressures from outside. Left to our own devices, we mess up. That's why we need help from beyond ourselves—a Saviour.

Spirituality isn't a branch of DIY.

1 PETER 5:8

Resisting the devil

Be self-controlled and alert. Your enemy the devil prowls around like a roaring lion looking for someone to devour.

If you mention the devil to most people, they think of a toasting fork, horns and cape; a comic book character in red tights and goatee beard. But as you read the Bible, you find a startling claim: there really is an invisible force of evil at work in the world, a force that goes beyond our own damaged human nature and the wrong values of society. If you tried to cut from the New Testament every passage on Satan and spiritual warfare, you would end up with a pile of confetti.

Having said that, we can safely throw out the horns and pitch-fork. Those were an invention of medieval artists. I grew up in the rationalistic 1970s, and was sure that the idea of the devil was superstitious nonsense. I knew that in a scientific culture like ours, nobody could believe in such a force in the world.

Now, I do believe in the devil. Not a devil with tights and horns. Not a 'personal' devil, either. God is personal, the source of life and personhood, and human beings made in God's image are personal. It is hard to see how a fallen spiritual being which has cut itself off from the source of personhood could be personal at all, since evil has no existence or creative power of its own: it is parasitic on goodness. I see the devil as an 'it' rather than a 'he': a drain, sucking away what's right and true; a disease that attacks a healthy body; a computer virus that corrupts a healthy hard-drive.

The good news is that the Bible says the devil's days are numbered. But for now, Peter's advice is as relevant today as it was in the first century: be self-controlled and alert.

Do I take seriously Jesus' warnings about the reality of evil in the world?

1 PETER 1:15

Reclaiming holiness

But just as he who called you is holy, so be holy in all you do.

Imagine we're together in a crowded room. I point across the room at someone and say, 'Look, there's a really *holy* person.' What sort of figure comes to mind? In my experience, most people picture a man standing alone, with a quiet voice and an awkward manner. In other words, a 'holy' person is introverted and antisocial!

There is no getting around it: in the Bible, followers of Jesus are called to be holy. But if we look at what holiness means in the Bible, it turns out to be something robust and positive. The word means 'set apart', or 'different'. That doesn't mean Christians are to be pulled out of the culture we live in, our workplaces and neighbourhoods. What sets us apart is having different priorities. You could define holiness as 'a positive alternative lifestyle'.

In Paul's letters, he often addresses his readers as 'saints', which means 'people who are already holy'. How can he do this, when they are clearly far from perfect? Paul explains the apparent paradox by using an image of clothing. He says that all who have become believers have 'clothed themselves' with Christ (Galatians 3:27). When God assesses our moral state, he sees only the qualities of his Son, who never fell flat on his face, messed up or compromised as we do. Instead of looking at our mistakes, God looks at Jesus and reckons to our account the holiness which is his.

But I still have a long way to go to experience as a daily reality the holiness that God sees when he looks at me, so holiness isn't only a gift that God gives me in Jesus. It is the process of growing into the hero I already am in God's eyes. You could say holiness is a process—of becoming what I am.

Lord, give me a compelling vision of holiness, and the commitment to make it real in my life.

MONDAY
---

1 CORINTHIANS 12:18–20 (ABRIDGED)

Part of the body

God has arranged the parts of the body… just as he wanted them to be. If they were all one part, where would the body be? As it is, there are many parts, but one body.

Christians are not supposed to be spiritual Lone Rangers. My faith should be personal, something I own with passion and commitment—but not private, a solitary hobby that I pursue in the privacy of my own home.

When I was baptized as a child, promises were made on my behalf about being a part of the Church. Confirmation means owning those promises for myself. I am part of both the universal and local church. Paul uses the image of a human body to illustrate what this means. A body is made up of many parts, each with a distinct role in the functioning of the body. In the same way, we are all different from one another but we all have our part to play in building up the life of the church.

Some people seem to believe they can follow Jesus without joining a local church. For others, going to church can feel isolating—rather like going to a cinema. When we visit the cinema, we are consumers of a show. We have little contact with the people sitting next to us, and we probably don't know them anyway. We go to have our emotions stirred by a performance, and then quietly slip away. Of course, if we don't like the film on offer in one cinema, we can visit a different one.

It's hard to imagine Paul recognizing this as church. To use Paul's analogy, if we go to church and fail to connect with other people, or if we avoid church altogether, we end up as severed body parts. A limb that's been cut off dies, and the body is weakened. A healthy body is one where every part is engaged and functioning.

In confirmation I commit myself to being a part of a body.

1 CORINTHIANS 12:28a

Discovering my gifts

In the church God has appointed first of all apostles, second prophets, third teachers, then workers of miracles, also those having gifts of healing, those able to help others, those with gifts of administration.

Paul talks about Christians as different parts of a body. To put it another way, we're all members of one family. There is an unmistakable family bond but we all have different personalities, outlooks and gifts. Part of my discipleship is discovering what distinctive gifts I bring to benefit the family.

Paul and Peter list examples of the kind of skills God gives people to help build up his church: wisdom, knowledge, faith, healing, miraculous powers, prophecy, discerning spirits, speaking in tongues and interpreting tongues (1 Corinthians 12:7–10); apostleship, teaching, helping and administration (v. 28); evangelism, pastoring (Ephesians 4:11); serving, encouraging, giving, leadership, showing mercy (Romans 12:7–8); hospitality, public speaking (1 Peter 4:9–11).

All Christians should ask what their spiritual gift is, and then develop it. How can we do that? We can ask others, and find out where they think we're gifted. We can try out different types of ministry and find what's a good fit. Lots of us have hidden abilities that we don't know about, because we've never really tried them. We can also look back over our lives: we may have learned lessons and skills from our own experiences (both positive and negative) that can help others. Another way to discern our gifts is simply to reflect on what we enjoy and find fulfilling. God wants us to play to our strengths: he gave us them in the first place.

What are my God-given gifts and skills?

1 CORINTHIANS 11:26

The family meal

*For whenever you eat this bread and drink this cup, you
proclaim the Lord's death until he comes.*

If the church is a family, with fellow Christians as brothers and
sisters, then the moment when the family gathers round a table
for a meal together is Holy Communion. This is one of two
'sacraments' instituted by Jesus, the other being baptism. A
sacrament has been defined as 'an outward and visible sign of an
inward and spiritual grace'. In other words, God takes mundane
things in the material world (water, bread, wine), and uses them
as a channel of spiritual blessing.

Confirmation has traditionally been the point where people can
receive bread and wine for the first time, and confirmation services
usually include Holy Communion. The ceremony always involves
retelling the story of the death and resurrection of Jesus, but it has
been given different names in different churches. Each of these
names can help us grasp a different aspect of what is going on.

'Communion' means 'fellowship' or sharing together, and
stresses the encounter between us and God, and between each
other, as we receive bread and wine.

'Eucharist' comes from a Greek word meaning 'to give thanks'.
We celebrate and give thanks for what God has done for us, and
will do in future.

'Mass' is from the closing words of the Latin Communion
service: '*ite, missa est*' ('Go, you are sent out'). The emphasis is on
being sent into the world to live for God.

The 'Lord's Supper' links our worship with the last meal that
Jesus shared with his followers. In Communion, we share in their
fellowship.

Ask God to make your experience of Holy Communion a powerful one.

1 CORINTHIANS 10:17

The meaning of Communion

*Because there is one loaf, we, who are many, are one body,
for we all partake of the one loaf.*

Holy Communion is 'quality time' with God and each other, but what is actually going on in the service? In Communion, we focus on what God has done for us in the past, will do in future, and what he is doing for us now.

Past: The Passover festival recalls God leading his people from slavery in Egypt. God had told the Hebrews to smear the blood of a lamb on their door-posts, so that when death visited Egyptian homes, it would avoid ('pass over') theirs. Passover celebrates a relationship with God made possible by the blood of a sacrificed lamb.

At the Last Supper, Jesus lifts a cup of wine representing the blood of the lamb, but says, 'This is my blood.' He himself is the sacrifice bringing salvation. Another element of Passover is unleavened (flat) bread. This represents the Israelites having to leave Egypt so quickly that their bread did not have time to rise. By taking the bread and saying, 'This is my body', Jesus was using the bread as a symbol of his own broken body.

Future: Jesus tells his disciples that the 'meal' they share is a foretaste of a future banquet with God in eternity. It is a deposit, a pledge of future riches (see Matthew 26:29).

Present: Communion is about meeting with Jesus Christ and other believers, here and now, and being strengthened to live for God today. We meet with Jesus; we also celebrate our unity with each other, symbolized in sharing one bread.

Our unity rests on Jesus Christ. How does that affect our attitude to church?

JOEL 2:28b

Dreams and visions

Your sons and daughters will prophesy, your old men will dream dreams, your young men will see visions.

I recently played 'word association' with friends: I'd say a word, and they'd shout other words or phrases that sprang to mind. When I said the word 'church', a high proportion of the words were negative. Their associations were either oppressive in some way ('dull', 'authoritarian', 'old-fashioned'), or they were to do with the building ('steeple', 'stained glass', 'font'), or else they were just mind-numbingly mundane ('tea and biscuits', 'the notices').

It got me thinking. The Jesus we meet in the Gospels is passionate, compelling and disturbing. His disciples abandoned everything to follow him. Jesus revolutionized their values and priorities, and modelled an intimacy with God that they had never dreamed of. Is it possible that this same Jesus sat down and thought, 'Now, what is going to be my legacy to the world? I know! A franchise in old buildings specializing in boredom and legalism!' I don't think so.

A few hundred years before Jesus, a prophet called Joel had a vision of a future day when the Spirit of God would come in power. People would have visions and dreams. It would be a time of excitement and wonder. Towards the end of his life, Jesus made an astounding promise: after he had left his friends, that same Spirit of God would finally come. Something dramatic was about to happen, in and through the church. The church should be a community that fills people with wonder and liberates creativity, a place where they can meet Jesus and find hope. At my confirmation I declare my commitment to that church, and I accept the job of helping it become the sort of church Jesus longs to see.

What will help my church become a place of dreamers and visionaries?

ACTS 6:6

Commissioning for action

They presented these men to the apostles, who prayed and laid their hands on them.

During the confirmation service; the bishop lays hands on each candidate and prays for them. What is going on here? The tradition of laying on hands goes back to biblical times, and has a number of meanings:

- *Giving authority for leadership:* For example, Moses commissions Joshua to lead the people (Numbers 27:23).
- *Blessing somebody:* Jacob (also known as Israel) lays his hands on his grandsons' heads to bless them (Genesis 48). Jesus blesses small children in the same way (Matthew 19:15).
- *Receiving the Holy Spirit or new spiritual gifts:* Peter and John rest their hands on believers so that they receive the Spirit (Acts 8:17). The young church leader Timothy has hands laid on him by elders of the church (1 Timothy 4:14).
- *Commissioning somebody for a special task:* The leaders of the early church commission seven people to oversee food distribution for needy widows, by laying hands on them (Acts 6:6). Later, Saul (soon to become Paul) and Barnabas have hands laid on them by the church leaders in Antioch (Acts 13:3), marking the start of their missionary work.

The common thread here is that praying for somebody as hands are laid on them acts as a channel for God's blessing or empowering for a particular task. At my confirmation the bishop prays that God will bless me and empower me for whatever plans and purposes God has in store for me.

How do I feel about God commissioning me to work for him in the world?

JOHN 20:22

The Holy Spirit

**And with that [Jesus] breathed on them and said,
'Receive the Holy Spirit.'**

In confirmation the bishop prays that God's Holy Spirit will rest on each candidate, and that they will receive more of the power of the Spirit. Clearly, this is a vital part of confirmation, but who or what is the Spirit? Biblically, the Holy Spirit is the invisible power and presence of God himself, at work in our world. That means the Holy Spirit is personal. To be a Christian means to have the Spirit of God at work in us.

Here are just a few examples of what the Spirit does. He draws us to God (1 Corinthians 2:12; 2 Thessalonians 2:13); he empowers us to tell others about Jesus Christ (Acts 2); he empowers us to live the Christian life (Galatians 5:16–26); he challenges us when we go wrong (Revelation 2:7, 29); he gives special 'gifts' for the mission of the church (1 Corinthians 12); he helps us worship God and pray (Romans 8:26); he brings unity between people (Ephesians 4:3–6). In other words, the Spirit is God's empowering presence, at work in our world, helping us to live the Christian life with greater effectiveness, joy and passion.

If those being confirmed are Christians (so the Spirit is already at work in them), why does the bishop need to pray for the Spirit? And why do church leaders invite the Spirit to come during times of worship, if he's already there? In practice, we are praying for more of God's Spirit, a greater measure. A leaf might be under the rays of the sun, but when the rays are focused with a magnifying glass, it will burn. We may have the Spirit, but we pray for a greater intensity of his presence at confirmation, in worship, and at our points of need.

Am I open to the work of God's Spirit in my life?

23

GALATIANS 5:22–23a

The fruit of the Spirit

The fruit of the Spirit is love, joy, peace, patience, kindness, goodness, faithfulness, gentleness and self-control.

One of the most important areas of the Spirit's work is in shaping our character. Paul talks about the 'fruit' of character that the Spirit grows in our lives, and, although he lists nine different varieties of 'fruit', he refers to them all together, in the singular. He assumes that the active presence of the Spirit will grow all nine in our lives, not just one or two. This fruit comes packaged in a gift hamper!

What does Paul's metaphor imply? Firstly, fruit grows on a tree and shows what kind of tree it is. And if the tree produces good fruit, it shows that the tree is healthy. Just before today's passage, Paul has given a list of bad fruit that evidences a sick tree, a life where the Spirit isn't present to bring health and vigour. Here, by contrast, is the fruit that indicates a healthy tree. The image of fruit further implies that change in my life is likely to be gradual rather than instant. Fruit ripens slowly.

How is God going to grow and ripen the fruit in our lives? Precisely by allowing us to be in situations where we're tempted to express an opposite reaction. Developing the fruit of the Spirit in our lives is a work that God does, but it's also a choice we make. For example, if I want to learn to be more loving, God may well put people around me whom I find hard to love. If I long to be more patient, I may find myself in situations when I'm forced to wait and confront my own temptation to be angry or impatient.

The Spirit is the one who grows the fruit of character in my life. He is also likely to lead me into situations where the fruit that's growing needs to be on display.

In which areas of my character do I need a fresh empowering by the Spirit of God?

PROVERBS 1:20

Real-world faith

Wisdom calls aloud in the street, she raises her voice in the public squares.

After confirmation, what next? The big question is what difference my faith is going to make to the rest of my life. It is easy to slip into a 'Sunday best' faith, which I only really think about when I'm in church. The real challenge is to live as a '24–7' Christian, somebody whose faith energizes and shapes a distinctive lifestyle. I need to address crucial life issues from the perspective of my faith. Here are a few to start with.

- *Priorities:* What matters most in my life? Am I giving enough time to what really matters? Have I got the balance right between family, work, social life, and church activities?
- *Decision-making:* How do I make decisions on big issues? Do I pray for God's guidance? Are there biblical insights on a particular issue?
- *Money/possessions:* How should I spend my money? How much should I give away—to church, and charity?
- *Relationships and sexuality:* Are my attitudes shaped more by the media, colleagues and the society around me, or by Christian assumptions? A Christian perspective would centre on faithfulness and commitment, and an understanding that adultery and other expressions of sex outside a lifetime commitment are inappropriate.
- *Character:* What sort of person am I? And what sort of person am I becoming? A useful checklist might be Paul's list of the 'fruit of the Spirit' that we have already looked at.

'The way people live is the best indication of what they really believe about reality—in contrast to what they may profess to believe' (Stanley Grenz, theologian and author).

2 TIMOTHY 3:16

Staying on track

All Scripture is God-breathed and is useful for teaching, rebuking, correcting and training in righteousness.

For some people, confirmation can be a spiritual high-point. They have been part of a preparation group, and enjoyed wrestling with questions of faith. The laying-on of hands and special prayers can be a powerful experience. But is it possible to stay close to God in the busyness of life, in a society that tends to squeeze God on to the sidelines?

Absolutely, but we need to be intentional about it. A crucial part of staying on track with God is building in time to read the Bible. After all, that's where we learn about Jesus' life and teaching, where we discover God's priorities. It is where we find inspiration and hope. The Christian faith has a 'Scripture principle': God has acted in history, and ensured that subsequent generations have a reliable account of his dealings with people. The Bible is a uniquely inspired interpretation of the meaning of history from beginning to end.

As we all know, though, many find the Bible impenetrable; others have used it to defend all kinds of oppression. Here are a few principles to bear in mind as you read. Make sure you have a Bible version that you understand. Ask: what would this passage have meant to its original hearers, and how does the style of the passage shape our understanding? You may need help from study notes. This prevents misunderstandings and the risk of reading in our own agendas. Don't just read individual verses, but build up a bigger picture by reading longer passages, or one of the shorter books at one sitting. Ask: what does this passage say to me? Be open to God speaking to you.

How can I make space in my schedule for Bible study?

1 PETER 4:12

When the going gets tough

*Dear friends, do not be surprised at the painful trial
you are suffering, as though something strange
were happening to you.*

Today's passage was written by Peter, about 30 years after the death and resurrection of Jesus, to encourage people going through tough times.

Life is bound to involve some degree of pain. It may be the pain when somebody close to us suffers and dies. It may be our own physical or emotional pain. It may be disappointment in life, a relationship that's damaged or broken, or disappointment in a job. For some, the fact that life contains hardship and suffering is the biggest obstacle to faith. This leads them to conclude that something has gone badly wrong, and they look for somebody to blame—doctors, the government, or God. They may decide that, in the words of Woody Allen, 'If there is a God, then basically he's an underachiever.'

Peter takes a startlingly different approach to life's trials. No, he says, nothing has gone wrong. To be human is to experience hard times. Does it mean God's not there? Not at all. Life includes pain. Peter and the other Bible writers don't give easy answers about why suffering exists, but they tell us something far more profound: God has entered into the suffering of the world in the person of Jesus, and experienced it first-hand. We worship a God who knows what pain feels like.

Where does my security lie? It can never depend on having a life insured against danger or suffering. Ultimately, my only security lies in having a Father who is trustworthy, who understands my pain, and will never abandon me.

God doesn't spare us from hardship—but he will be with us in it.

PSALM 23:1

The good shepherd

The Lord is my shepherd, I shall not be in want.
He makes me lie down in green pastures, he leads me
beside still waters.

Our last Bible reading is about the journey ahead—in particular, guidance and provision for the future. Psalm 23 draws on the image of the shepherd, who would have been a familiar sight throughout biblical times. God is described as being like a shepherd who provides us with green pastures (food). He leads us to still waters (drink). He leads us in right paths (guidance). He protects us from attacks in dark ravines ('valley of the shadow of death'). His strong staff urges us on, guides us and rescues us.

When we are young, our parents look after us. As we grow, we take greater responsibility for our own lives, and confirmation is an important part of taking responsibility for our faith. In these readings we have explored some of the challenges of developing a mature faith. In particular, we have used the language of being a disciple of Jesus. But we must never forget that discipleship was never meant to be a list of chores or duties. It isn't about striving to impress God or other people with our achievements. At its heart, being a disciple is about something much more simple and straightforward: following and trusting.

One of the most endearing characteristics of the shepherd in the ancient world was the closeness of his relationship with his flock. He had a distinctive call that his sheep would recognize, or a whistle tune he would play. The flock, in turn, knew who their shepherd was, and would only follow him.

Lord, I entrust my future into your hands. Lead me, guide me, protect and rescue me, I pray.

Bible reading notes from BRF

If you have found this booklet helpful and would like to continue reading the Bible regularly, you may like to explore BRF's three series of Bible reading notes.

NEW DAYLIGHT

New Daylight offers a devotional approach to reading the Bible. Each issue covers four months of daily Bible readings and reflection from a regular team of contributors, who represent a stimulating mix of church backgrounds. Each day's reading provides a Bible passage (text included), comment and prayer or thought for reflection. In *New Daylight* the Sundays and special festivals from the church calendar are noted on the relevant days, to help you appreciate the riches of the Christian year.

DAY BY DAY WITH GOD

Day by Day with God (published jointly with Christina Press) is written especially for women, with a regular team of contributors. Each four-monthly issue offers daily Bible readings, with key verses printed out, helpful comment, a prayer or reflection for the day ahead, and suggestions for further reading.

GUIDELINES

Guidelines is a unique Bible reading resource that offers four months of in-depth study written by leading scholars. Contributors are drawn from around the world, as well as the UK, and they represent a thought-provoking breadth of Christian tradition. *Guidelines* is written in weekly units consisting of six sections plus an introduction and a final section of points for thought and prayer.

If you would like to subscribe to one or more of these sets of Bible reading notes, please use the order form overleaf.

NOTES SUBSCRIPTIONS

❏ I would like to give a gift subscription (please complete both
   name and address sections below)
❏ I would like to take out a subscription myself (complete name
   and address details only once)

This completed coupon should be sent with appropriate payment to BRF.
Alternatively, please write to us quoting your name, address, the subscription
you would like for either yourself or a friend (with their name and address),
the start date and credit card number, expiry date and signature if paying by
credit card.

Gift subscription name _____

Gift subscription address_____

_____

_____Postcode _____

Please send beginning with the January / May / September issue:
(delete as applicable)

(please tick box)	UK	SURFACE	AIR MAIL
NEW DAYLIGHT	❏ £12.00	❏ £13.35	❏ £15.60
GUIDELINES	❏ £12.00	❏ £13.35	❏ £15.60
DAY BY DAY WITH GOD	❏ £12.75	❏ £14.10	❏ £16.35

Please complete the payment details below and send your coupon,
with appropriate payment to: **BRF, First Floor, Elsfield Hall, 15–17
Elsfield Way, Oxford OX2 8FG.**

Your name _____

Your address_____

_____

_____Postcode _____

Total enclosed £ _____ (cheques made payable to 'BRF')

Payment: cheque ❏ postal order ❏ Visa ❏ Mastercard ❏ Switch ❏

Card number: ☐☐☐☐☐☐☐☐☐☐☐☐☐☐☐☐☐☐

Expiry date of card: ☐☐☐☐ Issue number (Switch): ☐☐☐☐

Signature (essential if paying by credit/Switch card)

❏ Please do not send me further information about BRF publications.

BRF resources are available from your local Christian bookshop. BRF is a Registered Charity

Sometimes you need more than a card...

BIBLE READINGS FOR SPECIAL TIMES

Bereavement
Jean Watson

BIBLE READINGS FOR SPECIAL TIMES

Ill Health
Wendy Bray

BIBLE READINGS FOR SPECIAL TIMES

Marriage
Anna and Nick Brooker

BIBLE READINGS FOR SPECIAL TIMES

Retirement
David Winter

Confirmation
BIBLE READINGS FOR SPECIAL TIMES

Mike Starkey

Going to College
BIBLE READINGS FOR SPECIAL TIMES

Michael Volland

Moving House
BIBLE READINGS FOR SPECIAL TIMES

Catherine Hickey

New Baby
BIBLE READINGS FOR SPECIAL TIMES

Lindsay Melluish

Christian bookshops: All Christian bookshops stock BRF publications.
Telephone: To place your order, dial 01865 319700.
Fax: To place your order, dial 01865 319701.
Web: To place your order using the BRF website, visit www.brf.org.uk

REF	TITLE	PRICE	QTY	TOTAL
1 84101 418 4	Bible Readings for Special Times: Bereavement	£1.99		
1 84101 494 X	Bible Readings for Special Times: Confirmation	£1.99		
1 84101 447 8	Bible Readings for Special Times: Going to College	£1.99		
1 84101 421 4	Bible Readings for Special Times: Ill Health	£1.99		
1 84101 427 3	Bible Readings for Special Times: Marriage	£1.99		
1 84101 457 5	Bible Readings for Special Times: Moving House	£1.99		
1 84101 487 7	Bible Readings for Special Times: New Baby	£1.99		
1 84101 430 3	Bible Readings for Special Times: Retirement	£1.99		

POSTAGE & PACKING CHARGES				
Order value	UK	Europe	Surface	Air Mail
Under £7.00	£1.25	£3.00	£3.50	£5.50
£7.01–£29.99	£2.25	£5.50	£6.50	£10.00
Over £30.00	FREE	Prices on request		

Total Value of books	
Postage	
TOTAL	

Name _____

Account Number (if known) _____

Address _____

_____ Postcode _____

Telephone _____ Email _____

❐ Please email me with information about BRF resources and services

Method of payment:
❐ Cheque ❐ Mastercard ❐ Visa ❐ Postal Order ❐ Maestro

Card no.

☐☐☐☐ ☐☐☐☐ ☐☐☐☐ ☐☐☐☐ ▨▨▨

Issue no. of Switch card ☐☐☐   Expires ☐☐ ☐☐   *Shaded boxes for Maestro use only*

Signature _____

Date ___/___/___

All orders must be accompanied by the appropriate payment. Please make cheques payable to BRF.

Please send your completed form to:
brf, First Floor, Elsfield Hall, 15–17 Elsfield Way, Oxford OX2 8FG